Teleological
Argument and Responses
Advanced Higher
RMPS

Laura Crichton

Published 2024

ISBN: **9798328105330**

DEDICATION

For all RMPS teachers and their students

CONTENTS

1. Introduction — 1
2. Aquinas: argument from design — Pg 13
3. Paley: argument from design — Pg 28
4. Argument from intelligent design — Pg 52
5. Final thoughts and revision notes — Pg 65

1 INTRODUCTION

Imagine a situation where two people (say Ben and David) are locked away in separate rooms and told to create a pattern with 100 coloured marbles. However, while Ben is allowed to **design** this pattern by placing the marbles in a carefully thought-out plan, David is told that he must create randomly by continually throwing the marbles on the floor until a pattern is created **by chance**.

Ben of course does so very quickly. However, David takes 25 years. Nevertheless, his marbles (although differently arranged) clearly contain enough order to be described as a pattern.

Now given that you had no prior knowledge of the arrangements would it be possible to work out which of the patterns is DESIGNED and which is by CHANCE? Would there be any features in Ben's pattern that would distinguish it from David's pattern or vice versa?

Now these questions are very similar to those which are frequently asked of the Universe. The Universe (like the coloured marbles) clearly contains within it a great deal of order, pattern, and purpose (otherwise we wouldn't be here). Therefore, we are left to question whether:

1) The carefully worked out plan of a designer mind called God or

2) The result (for example) of Nature randomly throwing atoms around and eventually achieving this order, pattern, and purpose by chance.

Supporters of the teleological argument look at this dilemma and conclude that option 1) is the most sensible. Ultimately, they believe that the world we see around us just could not have arisen through chance occurrences.

In its simplest form, the teleological argument goes as follows:

- The universe has order, purpose and regularity. This can be seen in the way that the universe conforms to laws, and acts in a predictable manner.

- Had the universe been the product of chance, it is far more likely that it would have been chaotic.
- Therefore, such complexity is evidence of design, and this design implies a designer.
- Given the scale of the universe, that designer would possess divine intellect.
- This designer would traditionally be referred to as 'God'.

The word "teleological" comes from the Greek word *'teleos'* which means the purpose or end of something, but it is sometimes also referred to as the 'design argument.' It's basically about how we see order in the world and think it can't just be random—it must have been made that way on purpose. This isn't about saying 'God did it' right away, but it points to a designer who people traditionally identify as God.

By using scenarios such as the marble dilemma, the teleological argument asks the reader to draw upon their own experience of the world, and to apply this to the universe as a whole. To conclude that an intricate pattern could possibly be brought about by chance seemingly flies in the face of all rationality. But consider this - unlike a straightforward maths problem - this argument doesn't offer a definite answer but rather relies on clues to make an informed guess. It doesn't provide absolute certainty, but it does present a plausible inference. In essence, the design argument prompts us to recognize purposefulness in the world and proposes the existence of a designer behind it, despite not explicitly naming them as such.

The teleological argument rests upon *a posteriori* knowledge i.e. knowledge gained from our observations of the world. This is opposed to *a priori* knowledge, which is independent of observation and instead based on necessary truths – that hold true under all possible circumstances. Given that our understanding is constrained by our limited observations and experiences, the teleological argument is inherently **abductive**.

Abductive reasoning entails forming hypotheses to explain observed phenomena. In the case of the teleological argument, proponents analyse the intricacies and apparent design within the universe, inferring the existence of an intelligent designer. However, this inference is not deduced from strict logical necessity but rather from the plausibility drawn from observed patterns and structures. Thus, the teleological argument is best classified as abductive, as it seeks to explain the observed order and complexity of the universe by positing a designer.

Moreover, the teleological argument falls under the category of **inductive** arguments. Inductive arguments are based on observations and evidence, and their conclusions are not logically guaranteed, but rather supported by the available evidence. Any proponent must seek to a prove that a designer is the most likely solution. But if they wish to defend classical theism (i.e. the God of Christianity) they will need to show evidence that the designer is God.

Although there are different forms of teleological arguments, many also employ a form of argumentation based upon **analogy.** This is where two things are compared under the theory that they will also be alike in other (unobservable) ways too. For example, we can say that we know pupil X and pupil Y both attend the same school. We know that pupil X is going to university – we could draw the conclusion that since they have had the same schooling, that pupil Y will also be going to university… I can hear you thinking – "not necessarily" – and that's key! This analogy has obvious limitations, but let's think about the likelihood of it being true. If we could show that the vast majority of pupils from that school go to university, that surely would render the conclusion far more likely? It is also a destination that is often dependent on education – so it's not a particularly large logical jump to make. Whilst there is room for it to not be true, that's the flaw of all inductive argumentation - it does not result in philosophical truths. But the reality of the situation is that we live our lives based on induction. Very little in life can be absolutely guaranteed but our experience of the world informs our decisions on a daily basis; it's only in philosophy that we can mock someone for taking that approach.

Argument typology

Argument typology in philosophy refers to the categorization or classification of different types of arguments based on their structure, form, or content. It provides a systematic framework for understanding and analysing the various ways in which arguments can be constructed and evaluated. The design argument is both *inductive/abductive* and often *analogical*. One of the major philosophical criticisms of the argument is that employs both improperly.

💡 Reminder

1. Deduction:
    - Deduction is a logical process applicable to *a priori* truths – knowledge which is independent of our experience and observation.
    - Deductive reasoning guarantees the truth of its conclusion if the premises are true, and the reasoning is valid.
    - Conclusions are regarded as **necessarily** true or false such as the truths of pure mathematics.
    - Example: "A triangle has three sides"

2. Induction:
    - Induction is a form of reasoning where general conclusions are inferred from specific observations or evidence.

- Induction is the process application to *a posteriori* knowledge which is dependent upon our observations of the world.
- Inductive reasoning does not provide certainty; instead, it offers degrees of probability or likelihood.
- Example: "Every swan I have observed is white, so I conclude that all swans are white." This conclusion is based on observed instances and is likely to be true but not necessarily guaranteed, as there might be exceptions.

3. Abduction:
    - Abduction is a form of inference where the best explanation for observed evidence is sought, even if the explanation is not necessarily true.
    - Conclusions drawn through abduction are considered plausible or probable, rather than necessarily true or false.
    - Example: "If the grass is wet and there are dark clouds in the sky, it's likely that it has rained recently."

4. Analogy:
    - Analogical reasoning is a mode of thought where conclusions about one situation are drawn based on the similarity between that situation and another known situation.

- Analogical reasoning relies on the principle of applying what we know about one situation to another situation that shares relevant similarities.
- Analogical arguments don't yield absolute certainty; instead, they offer a level of confidence based on the degree of similarity between the situations being compared.
- Example: "Since cats and lions are both felines and cats are domesticated animals, it's likely that lions can also be domesticated." This conclusion draws on the similarity between cats and lions as felines, but it's not guaranteed as there could be differences in behaviour or other factors between the two species.

Identify whether the following arguments are inductive, abductive, or deductive, and which employ analogy.

1. Every time I eat strawberries, I get a rash. Strawberries and Bananas are both fruit. Therefore, bananas will cause me to have a rash.
2. All squares have four equal sides, and this shape has four equal sides. Therefore, this shape is a square.
3. Every time I press the button, the light turns on. Therefore, pressing the button causes the light to turn on.
4. All mammals are warm-blooded, and a bat is a mammal. Therefore, a bat is warm-blooded.

5. Based on the past 100 years of data, we predict that the stock market will increase in value next year.
6. Cats have tails and make great pets. Rats also have tails. Therefore, rats make great pets.
7. All observed instances of consuming sugar lead to increased energy levels. Therefore, consuming sugar probably boosts energy.
8. From observing the behaviour of this species of bird, we hypothesize that it migrates south for the winter.
9. If it's raining outside, then the ground will be wet. It's raining outside. Therefore, the ground is wet.
10. Every time I water the plant, it grows taller. Therefore, watering the plant likely contributes to its growth.

To make a brief in-juncture at this point, as we're making the leap up to Advanced Higher, we need to make use of the Latin term *Qua* meaning 'as relating to' - so we're talking about the design argument in two parts - design *qua* regularity and design *qua* purpose.

"Design qua regularity" specifically focuses on the regular patterns and laws observed in the universe. Advocates of the teleological argument argue that these regularities are not merely random occurrences but instead reflect a purposeful arrangement that points towards an intelligent designer. They argue that the consistency and predictability of natural laws, as well as the finely-tuned parameters of the universe, suggest intentional design rather than mere chance.

One of the most cited examples of fine-tuning involves the physical constants of the universe. These constants, such as the gravitational constant, the speed of light, and the strength of electromagnetism, are precisely set to values that allow for the existence of life. If these constants were even slightly different, the universe would not be capable of supporting life as we know it. For instance, if the gravitational constant were slightly stronger or weaker, stars and galaxies might not have formed, or chemical elements necessary for life might not have been synthesized in sufficient quantities.

"Design qua purpose" refers to the aspect of the teleological argument that focuses on the apparent purpose or goal-directedness observed in the universe. In this instance, proponents highlight features of the universe such as living organisms, which exhibit characteristics that suggest they were designed with a specific purpose in mind. For example, the human eye is often cited as an example of complex design, with its various components finely tuned to allow for vision.

Thinking Task – IS THE FIBONACCI SEQUENCE EVIDENCE OF DESIGN?

What is the next number? 1, 1, 2, 3, 5, 8, 21, 34, 55 ....

Named after the Italian mathematician Leonardo of Pisa, who was known as Fibonacci, this sequence frequently appears in various natural phenomena, such as the branching of trees, the arrangement of leaves on a stem, the spirals of a pinecone, the pattern of seeds in a sunflower, and spirals of shells. It also has numerous applications in mathematics and computer science, particularly in algorithms, number theory, and even cryptography. The ratio between successive Fibonacci numbers converges to the golden ratio, a mathematical constant approximately equal to 1.618, which further enhances the sequence's significance in art, architecture, and design. The prevalence of the Fibonacci sequence across diverse domains of naturehas led many to view it as evidence of a deliberate design or underlying order in the universe – rather like God has left his 'fingerprint' on creation

What do you think?

A quick note about syllogisms

In the next chapter, we'll be using the word 'syllogism'. If this is a new term for you, then this is the page for you.

A syllogism is a form of logical reasoning where a conclusion is drawn from two given or assumed propositions (premises). Each premise shares a common term with the conclusion, leading to a logical connection. The basic structure involves a major premise, a minor premise, and a conclusion. For example:

1. Major premise: All humans are mortal.
2. Minor premise: Socrates is a human.
3. Conclusion: Therefore, Socrates is mortal.

This classic syllogism demonstrates how two premises can lead to a logical and valid conclusion. Provided the premises are true, and the logic is sound, then one can conclude that the conclusion is valid.

✎ Now try to create some syllogisms of your own.

2 AQUINAS: ARGUMENT FROM DESIGN

The fifth way is taken from the governance of the world. We see that things which lack intelligence, such as natural bodies, act for an end, and this is evident from their acting always, or nearly always, in the same way, so as to obtain the best result. Hence it is plain that not fortuitously, but designedly, do they achieve their end. Now whatever lacks intelligence cannot move towards an end, unless it be directed by some being endowed with knowledge and intelligence; as the arrow is shot to its mark by the archer. Therefore some intelligent being exists, by whom all natural things are directed to their end, and this being we call God.[1]

---

[1] An Extract from Aquinas' *Summa Theologiae*, Part a, 2, 3. (London, Eyre & Spottiswoode, 1972).

Thomas Aquinas, a prominent medieval theologian, presented several influential arguments for the existence of God in his monumental work, *Summa Theologica*. Although this text was unfinished, Aquinas systematically addresses various theological questions, including the nature of God and the purpose of human existence.

Summa Theologica is basically a manual for beginners in theology and a collection of all the main theological teachings of the Church. It presents the reasoning for almost all points of Christian theology in the West. The *Summas* topics follow a cycle – the existence of God, Creation, Man, Man's purpose, Christ, the Sacraments... and back to God.

Among his notable contributions are the *Quinque Viae*, or Five Ways, which are arguments for the existence of God. It is Aquinas' fifth argument that we turn to for his teleological argument – 'from the governance of things.' Aquinas' argument centres on the observable order and purposefulness in the universe. In simple terms, he observed that things in the universe seem to behave in a purposeful and orderly manner. Think about how seeds grow into plants when given sunlight and water, or how the Earth consistently rotates, giving us day and night. Everywhere we look, from the smallest organisms to the largest celestial bodies, there's a remarkable consistency in their behaviour.

Aquinas pointed out that this consistent behaviour implies a kind of goal-directedness or purposefulness (design *qua* purpose) For instance, a seed "knows" how to grow into a plant, following a specific pattern to achieve that end. However, these objects—like seeds, planets, and natural phenomena—lack minds or intelligence. Yet, they seem to act as if they have a purpose or goal in mind.

Aquinas further developed his argument through the analogy of an archer firing an arrow; "nothing lacking awareness can tend to a goal except it be directed by someone with awareness and understanding; the arrow, for example, requires an archer".[2] The arrow is non-sentient and lacks awareness, he argues, yet is being directed by the archer for a purpose - to hit a target. For the arrow can only be given a purpose if there is a being with awareness (the archer) who can direct it. He suggests that, in the same way, the universe lacks awareness and sentience and can only perform a purpose (e.g. sustaining life) if there is something with awareness that directs it. This must be God.

---

[2] Stanley Tweyman. *David Hume: Critical Assessments, Volume 5.* (London, 1995). 200

To express Aquinas' argument as a syllogism:

P1: Things that lack intelligence, such as living organisms, act for an end (i.e. they behave in a purposeful way).

P2: Natural objects lack intelligence, and therefore cannot move unless they are directed by an intelligent being.

P3. For example, an arrow does not direct itself towards its target, it needs an archer to aim and fire.

C: Therefore, there must be an intelligent designer guiding the behaviour of natural objects, whom we identify as God.

Thinking Questions

As Aquinas' argument relies on empirical observation, what type of knowledge is this?

He reasoned that since natural objects lack intelligence yet behave purposefully, there must be an external intelligence guiding them towards their ends. What type of logic did Aquinas employ here?

Aquinas compared an archer aiming an arrow at a target to natural objects also achieving an end. What type of argument is this and what limitations does it have?

Philosophical Responses

The key attacking syllogisms is to either show that one of the premises is false, or that incorrect logic has been utilised. So let us look at each premise in turn:

P1: Things that lack intelligence, such as living organisms, act for an end (i.e. they behave in a purposeful way).

This statement is not *necessarily* false, but it is an oversimplification in that it does not accurately capture the complexities of how living organisms behave. Realistically, not all behaviour is purposeful in that not all actions are driven by conscious intention or directed towards a specific end. Many behaviours in living organisms can be explained through biological processes.

P2: Natural objects lack intelligence, and therefore cannot move unless they are directed by an intelligent being.

Again, this isn't necessarily false, but it also isn't necessarily true! Just because we currently lack a complete naturalistic explanation does not mean that there isn't one. It may fairly be described as an 'argument of ignorance.' This fallacy occurs when someone asserts that a proposition is true because it has not been proven false or vice versa. In this instance, it may be that science one day will be able to help use to explain how natural objects move without intelligence, but for now to simply use God to 'fill in the gaps' isn't the answer.

Inductive arguments like this one rely on us using our experience to form the most likely conclusion. In this instance, one can argue that there were once many things that we could not explain – such as the changing weather – that people attributed to God. Science has slowly been able to explain all those phenomena so it is reasonable to assume that the remaining 'gaps' in our knowledge will also one day have an answer. To say 'God did it' is just a temporary stop gap.

P3. For example, an arrow does not direct itself towards its target, it needs an archer to aim and fire.

Whilst premise three is undoubtably true, one can question whether it is a good analogical comparison. Dr Robert Hambourger, a philosophy professor who spent most of his career at NC State University, wrote that analogous design arguments constrain and reduce nature, because they suggest that nature is like man-made objects and artifacts. He went on to say that random processes could create a universe with complex and beautiful structures: they might come about rarely and remain, whereas ugly and dysfunctional structures may die away. The archer analogy fails to acknowledge that just as an arrow can sometimes miss its mark due to a poor archer, nature can also fail, and we see species die out. If we were to follow the analogy through to its logical limits one would have to conclude that the designer was not very good.

C: Therefore, there must be an intelligent designer guiding the behaviour of natural objects, whom we identify as God.

Finally, we have the conclusion which allows us to see an additional problem with premise 2 in that Aquinas has employed circular reasoning. Premise 2 stated that natural objects cannot move without an intelligent being directing them however, he is also concluding that there must be an intelligent being. Aquinas assumed (in premise 2) the very conclusion he was trying to prove. This circular reason is sometimes called the **fallacy of begging the question.**

Scientific responses

As we've already discussed, one criticism that can be levelled at Aquinas is that he simply filled his lack of awareness of science with God i.e. his God is a 'God of the gaps.' Modern critics would point out that the apparent design that Aquinas saw in the world was not as it seems. Evolutionary theory provides a naturalistic explanation for the apparent design in living organisms.

Through the mechanism of natural selection acting on random variations (mutations), complex and seemingly purposeful features can arise without the need for a guiding intelligence. Evolution is any change across successive generations in the heritable characteristics of biological populations. Evolutionary processes give rise to diversity at every level of biological organization, including species, individual organisms, and molecules such as DNA and proteins.

The theory follows that life on Earth originated and then evolved from a universal common ancestor approximately 3.7 billion years ago. Repeated speciation and the divergence of life can be traced through shared sets of biochemical and morphological traits, or by shared DNA sequences. These homologous traits and sequences are more similar among species that share a more recent common ancestor, and can be used to reconstruct evolutionary histories, using both existing species and the fossil record. Existing patterns of biodiversity have been shaped both by speciation and by extinction.

Charles Darwin was the first to formulate a compelling scientific argument for the theory of evolution by means of natural selection. Evolution by natural selection is a population level process that is inferred from three facts:

1) More offspring are produced than can possibly survive,

2) Traits vary among individuals, leading to differential rates of survival and reproduction, and

3) Trait differences are heritable.

Thus, when members of a population die, they are replaced by individuals that are not born from random parents. Instead, these new members are born from parents that are better adapted to the environment in which natural selection took place. This can cause the evolution of traits that are seemingly fitted for the functional roles they perform. Natural selection is the only known cause of adaptation, but not the only known cause of evolution. Other, nonadaptive causes of evolution include mutation and genetic drift.

In the early 20th century, genetics was integrated with Darwin's theory of evolution by natural selection through the discipline of population genetics. The importance of natural selection as a cause of evolution was accepted into other branches of biology. Moreover, previously held notions about evolution, such as orthogenesis and "progress" became obsolete. Scientists continue to study evolution by constructing theories, by using observational data, and by performing experiments in both the field and the laboratory. Biologists agree that descent with modification is one of the most reliably established facts in science. Discoveries in evolutionary biology have made a significant impact not just within the traditional branches of biology, but also in other academic disciplines (e.g., anthropology and psychology) and on society at large.

It's important to note that evolution is a theory that is based upon observation, that makes it *a posteriori* and it is also an inductive argument. So just as Aquinas' premises can be criticized for not *necessarily* being true, so too can evolution. The key difference is that proponents of evolution have found evidence to strengthen its case, such as fossil records, genetic similarities among different species, and observed instances of natural selection. To be fair it's also an argument that has been horribly mischaracterized by the theists who proclaim that it's a ridiculous theory i.e. there was nothing and then bang through chance we had humans! That's simply not the case. It's one small mutation after another, and after another.

As Dawkins wrote in 'The Blind Watchmaker': life has the creative potential within itself and takes the opportunity afforded it by genetic mutation to actualize its potential. God is not needed to explain this – it is self-explanatory.

If we are being fair to Aquinas, he was not aware of this level of science – and nor could he be. The theory of evolution was developed centuries after his death;

other more modern proponents of teleological arguments don't have this excuse!

Religious responses

In 2009, the Vatican admitted that Darwin's theory of evolution should not have been dismissed and claimed it is compatible with the Christian view of Creation. Archbishop Gianfranco Ravasi, head of the Pontifical Council for Culture, said while the Church had been hostile to Darwin's theory in the past, the idea of evolution could be traced to St Augustine and St Thomas Aquinas. Father Giuseppe Tanzella-Nitti, Professor of Theology at the Pontifical Santa Croce University in Rome, added that 4th century theologian St Augustine had "never heard the term evolution, but knew that big fish eat smaller fish" and forms of life had been transformed "slowly over time" and argued that Aquinas made similar observations in the Middle Ages. Monsignor Ravasi said Darwin's theories had never been formally condemned by the Roman Catholic Church, pointing to comments more than 50 years ago, when Pope Pius XII described evolution as a valid scientific approach to the development of humans.[3]

---

[3] https://www.telegraph.co.uk/news/religion/4588289/The-Vatican-claims-Darwins-theory-of-evolution-is-compatible-with-Christianity.html

Today, the Church's unofficial position is an example of theistic evolution, also known as evolutionary creation, stating that faith and scientific findings regarding human evolution are not in conflict, though humans are regarded as a special creation, and that the existence of God is required to explain both monogenism and the spiritual component of human origins. In short, theistic evolutionists believe that there is a God; that God is the creator of the material universe and (by consequence) all life within, and that biological evolution is simply a natural process within that creation. Evolution, according to this view, is simply a tool that God employed to develop human life. They have not abandoned Aquinas' idea that God is still guiding the arrow to its target!

In his book *Philosophical Theology*, British philosopher FR Tennant picks up on this point and argues that the apparent purpose of evolution allows the design argument to work, as it appears to be directed by intelligence. If something is moving toward a goal, then there must be a guiding hand. His point is simple: had there been minute changes in the values of the forces responsible for the development of the world and life, then it would be very unlikely that anything would have developed at all. In his opinion, God is responsible for this fine-tuning. A similar point is also found in Hugh Montefiore's book, the Probability of God who continues this line of argument by saying 'the distribution of gas in the universe from the big bang onwards had to be delicately balanced... without this fine balance, there would have been no galaxies, no starts, no planets, no life.'

Tennant also challenged the theory of evolution by saying that there are many aspects of human nature that have no evolutionary advantage. Natural selection simply cannot account for man's capacity for 'aesthetic awareness'. He argues that people are beyond where they would have naturally evolved to. This, he argues, can only be explained as a function of revelation, which in turn suggests the 'invisible and mysterious presence' of God. Similar arguments are also found in the work of AE Taylor and Peter Bertocci. Taylor argues that human intelligence transcends natural selection and cannot therefore be accounted for. Bertocci, following Tennant, concentrates on man's artistic capacities. For him, the artist is a man responding to nature, revealing nature to others, making apparent in artistic form a relation already presupposed between man and his environment. This interconnection between human beings and the natural world is, he claims, inexplicable without postulating a designing intelligence, who has established this interaction and fundamental harmony.

Thinking Task

Imagine you travel back in time and meet Thomas Aquinas. He tries out his argument on you and is wondering whether to include it in his book.

How would you reply and why?

Past Paper Question 2021: Source Question

'Some intelligent being exists, by whom all natural things are directed to their end.' 'Summa Theologica', Thomas Aquinas

(a) Describe what is meant by the argument from design. (5)

This question isn't asking you to directly respond to the source, but it is giving you an indication of the topic. Respond to this with factual information. You should be able to do this in approximately five sentences.

(b) Analyse this source. (5)

This is asking you about the source – NOT the topic. Analysis is about thinking about the implications or potential issues that could arise. For this example, think about what you know about the Author – what potential bias could he have? What type of argumentation is being employed – does this have any potential limits? What other views might the author hold given what they have written?

(c) Evaluate this source. (5)

This question is asking you to provide a justified judgement as to whether you agree with the source. You can offer argument in both support and/or disagreement.

3 PALEY: ARGUMENT FROM DESIGN

In crossing a heath, suppose I pitched my foot against a stone and were asked how the stone came to be there, I might possibly answer that for anything I knew to the contrary it had lain there forever; nor would it, perhaps, be very easy to show the absurdity of this answer. But suppose I had found a watch upon the ground, and it should be inquired how the watch happened to be in that place, I should hardly think of the answer which I had before given, that for anything I knew the watch might have always been there. Yet why should not this answer serve for the watch as well as for the stone?[4]

---

[4] An extract from William Paley's "Natural Theology" published in 1802

William Paley was an 18th century English Christian apologist, his means that he aimed to provide a rational basis for Christian faith. In 1802 he put forward his design argument in his book, *Natural Theology*. He employed an **analogical argument** in which he proposed that if we were to come across a watch, we would note that it is very complex because it is composed of many different parts and it has an obvious purpose i.e. to tell the time. We can assume that the watch did not come into existence by chance and that it was designed by a watchmaker; as Paley postulated, "the watch must have had a maker... there must have existed at some time, and at some place or other, an artifice or artificers, who formed it for the purpose... and designed its use"[5]. If we look at the universe in the same way, it is also undoubtedly very complex and has a purpose; to sustain life. Therefore, it is reasonable to infer that the universe also has a designer.

There are a couple things to note here, we may scoff at the idea of comparing a watch to the universe, but Paley was not being original in his thought here. Watches and timepieces have been used as examples of complicated technology in philosophical discussions throughout history. Cicero, Voltaire, and René Descartes, for example, used timepieces in arguments regarding purpose. The watchmaker analogy was first used by Fontenelle in 1686 but Paley is the one who has become known for it.

---

[5] Michael Palmer. *The Question of God.* (London: Routledge, 2001). 145

A reminder here, that analogy (as a form of induction) is an argument based on resemblances. There resemblances can be used to support additional claims that these instances further resemble each other in ways that are not immediately observable or testable. These assumptions, however, are not conclusive. To assume that there are, is to commit a well-known logical error – **the fallacy of the affirmation of the consequent** – our favourite example being: When Laura drinks coffee she is happy, Laura is happy, therefore Laura must have drunk coffee. But there are other things that make Laura happy (like cinnamon buns!) so to ignore this fact is to commit the fallacy.

Therefore, any analogy could have this problem: like effects may not have like causes.

Let's dive back into Paley's argument. He firstly supported his analogy by focusing on 'design qua purpose' (remember, this means design as relating to purpose). Paley looked closely at the eye and how its different parts collaborate to make vision possible. He was convinced that the eye's intricate design couldn't have just happened randomly—it seemed perfectly crafted for the sole purpose of seeing. This, he believed, strongly hinted at the involvement of an intelligent creator. Paley also pointed to other examples in nature, like birds' wings and fish fins, which seemed tailor-made for their specific functions. To him, all this evidence pointed to one conclusion: a designer—whom Paley identified as God—must have been behind it all.

But Paley then also focused on 'design qua regularity.' Paley used evidence from astronomy and Newton's laws of motion and gravity to prove that there is design in the universe. Paley pointed to the rotation of the planets in the solar system, and how they obey the same universal laws, and hold their orbits because of gravity. This could not have come about by chance. He concluded that an external agent must have imposed order on the universe as a whole and on its many parts, and that this agent must be God.

This is a good point to discuss the idea of proportion. To summarise, Paley has suggested that since the effects of human contrivance are so similar to the regularities we see in nature and the purposeful mechanisms found in the natural world, we may legitimately infer that the causes which produce these effects are similarly alike. Moreover, the complexity of the universe far exceeds the complexity of anything man-made (like a pocket watch). Therefore, we may further infer that the designer of the universe far exceeds in intelligence any human designer. The designer of the universe, therefore, must possess a divine intelligence. And if the universe is more complex than man-made artefacts, it would be absurd to suggest it came about by chance!

Thinking Task

What is your emotional response to the images?
Can you infer any *conclusions* from the images? If so, what are they?
Is it in human nature to interpret these images in the same or similar way?

'Inference' is the process of deriving conclusions from what is known or assumed to be true.

What (if anything) can you infer about the producer of the following objects?

Philosophical responses

In his 'Dialogues Concerning Natural Religion', David Hume offers a renowned encapsulation of the Design Argument, along with its notable critique. Notably, Hume predated Paley's argument by 22 years, illustrating a gap between philosophy and theology. It's not known whether Paley was aware of Hume's writing, because although he does address some of the criticisms there are others that are unanswered. Conversely, Hume demonstrates awareness of Paley's argument, even contemplating the analogy of a watch. As we mentioned before – the use of a watch analogy was not new!

In *Dialogues* Hume presents a conversation between three characters:

- Cleanthes, an advocate of Natural Theology who presents arguments for God's existence based on empirical evidence.
- Demea, who shares belief in God but relies on a priori reasoning for his arguments.
- Philo, their critic, who most people assume is Hume's own viewpoint.

Hume was critical of certain religious doctrines and arguments for the existence of God, particularly those based on traditional metaphysical reasoning or empirical observations, but he did not outright identify as an atheist. Instead, he often described himself as a sceptic or agnostic. The character Philo is used by Hume to mock Cleanthes and Demea and seeks to destroy the basis for their belief – hence most people believe this is a reflection of Hume's own scepticism.

The uniqueness of the Universe

Hume argues that analogical arguments rely on demonstrating resemblances, the stronger the resemblance, the stronger the argument. Conversely, the greater the difference, the more implausible any analogical inference becomes. His point is straightforward: comparing the universe to a man-made artifact is ludicrous, as Hume points out to Cleanthes, stating, "The dissimilitude is so striking that the utmost you can pretend to is a guess, a conjecture, a presumption concerning a similar cause; and how that pretension will be received in the world, I leave you to consider."

Hume contends that this tendency is a "determination of the mind" stemming from our inclination towards explanation. Moreover, he asserts that an effective analogy necessitates examining multiple instances of the objects being compared. However, the universe is unique—it is neither an artifact like a watch, nor an organ like an eye, nor an organism like a monkey. Given our lack of comparable entities, analogy becomes inapplicable. The only scenario in which analogy could be useful is if we had other universes for comparison, which would require firsthand experience of their origins.

Hume goes highlight that the teleological argument falls into the 'fallacy of the affirmation of the consequent.' This is a logical error that occurs when someone assumes that if a certain condition (the consequent) is true, then its cause or antecedent must also be true. For example, Paley arguable committed this error by assuming that 'universal' laws, such as gravity, apply uniformly everywhere for all time. Hume argues against this assumption due to the *a posteriori* nature of the argument, emphasizing our limited experience of the universe and the potential variation in these laws elsewhere. As Hume writes, there is no justification for assuming "that instances of which we have had no experience must resemble those of which we have had experience."

Checking Understanding

1. What are the key components of Hume's critique of analogical arguments, particularly in the context of comparing the universe to man-made artifacts?
2. How does Hume's concept of "determination of the mind" influence our inclination to make analogical inferences?
3. What is the "fallacy of the affirmation of the consequent" and how does Hume apply it to Paley's teleological argument?
4. How does Hume's emphasis on the *a posteriori* nature of the argument challenge assumptions about universal laws like gravity?
5. Considering Hume's critique, how might proponents of the teleological argument respond to his objections?

The diversity of causal explanations

Even if we were to reject the initial aspect of Hume's argument—assuming, for the moment, that the analogy between the world and an artifact validates the conclusion that the world has a designer—the subsequent phase of his argument, often considered more devastating, further diminishes this possibility.

Let's revisit the scenario of David and his marbles from the very first chapter. Imagine that the only instance you enter his room is during the 25th year, precisely when he manages to create a pattern with the marbles through a chance throw. In this situation, you might be inclined to think that the pattern on the floor could only have been created by design. This inclination arises because you were not present during David's 15 billion throws of the marbles, which only resulted in chaos.

Hume's argument posits that any universe would give the appearance of being designed, even if it were not. To assume that order and purpose can only arise through design is to commit the 'fallacy of the affirmation of the consequent'—the effects we observe could have various causes.

Hence, Hume proceeds to offer two alternative explanations for the appearance of design. Firstly, he considers the possibility that order and design, while resembling the effects of human activity, may more closely resemble the effects achieved by the biological activities of animals and plants. Here, principles such as instinct, generation, and vegetation operate to produce an ordered world without any external intelligent agency. Why not conceive of this planetary system as a 'great vegetable' producing 'certain seeds within itself, which, when scattered into the surrounding chaos, vegetate into a new world?' Why not view the world as an 'Animal,' with a comet as its egg? Why not endorse the notion that 'the world arose from an infinite spider, who spun this whole complicated mass from his bowels?'

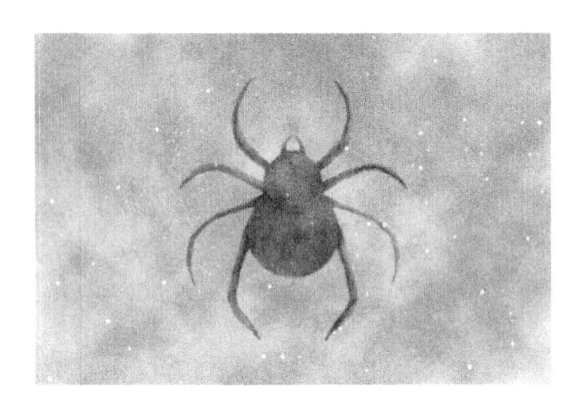

While these alternatives reflect Hume's mocking tone, they cannot simply be dismissed, as Demea would have us do, solely on the grounds of lacking evidence. We are dealing with rival theories concerning the causes of order in nature. One theory suggests a designing intelligence based on human effects, while the other proposes natural self-regulation and growth based on biological effects. If one theory is rejected due to lack of evidence, there is no reason why we cannot reject the other on the same grounds. As Hume writes, 'Our experience, so imperfect in itself, and so limited both in extent and duration, can afford us no probable conjecture concerning the whole of things. But if we must needs fix on some hypothesis; by what rule, pray, ought we to determine our choice?'
This criticism is not lost on Cleanthes, who, while asserting that Philo's objections defy sense and reason,

concedes that he cannot yet provide a satisfactory answer to them.

Hume acknowledges that his second explanation for the appearance, if not the fact, of design is similarly fanciful. However, its absurdity is irrelevant. What must be established is whether it is any less absurd than the theistic alternative. Thus, based on the evidence before us, it is plausible to offer a thoroughly materialistic and mechanistic interpretation of the world. For all we know, the order we observe could result from the chance collisions of particles of matter, without any guiding intelligence.

Hume's perspective is that Nature, like David, continuously throws particles around in unlimited time. Eventually, one of these chance throws produces a pattern that allows life to emerge and produce creatures like us. When we arrive on the scene, we are tempted to be impressed by the pattern we see in the Universe and to conclude that it could only have been created by design. However, according to Hume, this conclusion arises because we were not present during Nature's many other throws of the particles, which only resulted in chaos. Chaotic combinations of particles never produce creations like ourselves. Therefore, we only emerge on the scene when a complex pattern has been thrown by nature because only this sort of pattern allows us to exist.

This aligns with the Epicurean hypothesis, proposed by the Greek philosopher Epicurus of Samos. Epicurus' account of physical nature postulates a universe infinite in extent, without beginning or end, evolving from a primordial and immeasurable plurality of uncreated and indivisible particles. The world was not created by gods or designed by them for some ultimate purpose—the gods themselves are seen as the products of the material universe and completely indifferent to its functioning. Changes occur as a result of accidental collisions or 'swerves' of these atomic particles.

Hume poses the question, 'the eternal revolutions of unguided matter, and may not this account for all the appearing wisdom and contrivance, which is in the universe?' Perhaps the order in the universe is merely a perception of our human minds, attempting to impose order on something that simply exists. This parallels the marble scenario—our minds are inclined to think that David designed his pattern, despite lacking evidence.

In conclusion, we are presented with two rival hypotheses: authentic design (the universe is the product of intelligent design) and apparent design (the universe appears designed but is not). The evidence, namely the order in the universe, is ambiguous and provides no compelling reason to favour the theistic solution over other explanations for the order of the universe.

Checking Understanding

1. Explain what is meant by the: 'fallacy of the affirmation of the consequent'.
2. Do you think that Paley is guilty of committing this fallacy?

3. How do scientific responses, such as those explored in the last chapter i.e. the theory of evolution, impact this criticism?

The principle of proportionality

Hume revisits his critique of analogy, now focusing on the inductive principle of proportionality: like effects suggesting like causes.

Even if we accept the analogy between human artifacts and the universe as indicative of a designing intelligence, Hume argues it doesn't provide sufficient grounds for religious conclusions about God's nature. He insists that attributing qualities to God must be exactly sufficient to produce the observed effects, which raises questions about the nature and attributes of God inferred from the design argument. Philo's rant at this point is rather fun:

> "This world, for aught he knows, is very faulty and imperfect, compared to a superior

standard; and was only the first rude essay of some infant deity, who afterwards abandoned it, ashamed of his lame performance: it is the work only of some dependent, inferior deity; and is the object of derision to his superiors: it is the production of old age and dotage in some superannuated deity; and ever since his death, has run on at adventures, from the first impulse and active force which it received from him."

Hume is not explicitly denying that the design argument works. Rather, he contends that if it does work, it leads to the conception of a limited, anthropomorphic, and imperfect God. As a result, Hume presents three different alternatives:

1. If we look at the vast diversity within the universe, and the supposed 'complexity.' Is if not more reasonable to suppose that a team of Deities were responsible? Just as a 'a great number of men join in building a house or ship.'

2. His second possibility is that God has ceased to exist – a designer does not need to outlive their design.

3. Finally, why not extend the analogy to imagine a God with a human figure?

Hume is leaving us to imagine (if successful) the teleological argument can only possibly prove an inept designer.

We need to be fair to Paley here and highlight that he did attempt to deal with this criticism. There is some debate over whether he was aware of Hume's work, but certainly, people would've been discussing the general idea of the design argument at that time, and Paley would've been aware of such criticisms.

In the opening chapter of *Natural Theology*, Paley emphasized that even if we've never witnessed the creation of a watch and lack the ability to do so ourselves, or if we cannot grasp the process involved, and even if the watch occasionally malfunctions or contains defective parts, these factors do not negate the existence of a designer. If anything, it just makes the ability to design a watch more impressive – and even more so a universe! Paley accepts that faults may not lead to the God of Classical Theism, but maintains that none of these elements actually preclude a creator or designer.

Many have accused Paley of then ignoring the analogical inference here, that it can only lead to a God that's inept and unworthy of worship. But Paley does come back to address this point in his 5th chapter:

> ...*we must also judge of his intention, and of the provisions employed in fulfilling that*

intention, not from an instant in which they fail, but from the great plurality of instances in which they succeed. But, after all, these are different questions from the question of the artist's existence: or, which is the same, whether the thing before us be a work of art or not; and the questions ought always to be kept separate in the mind... Irregularities and imperfections are of little or no weight in the consideration, when that consideration relates to simply to the existence of a Creator. When the argument respects his attributes, they are of weight; but are then to be taken in conjunction... with the unexceptionable evidences which we possess, of skill, power, and benevolence, displayed in other instances; which evidences may, in strength, number, and variety, be such, and may so overpower, apparent blemishes, as to induce us, upon the most reasonable ground, to believe, that these last ought to be referred to some cause, though we be ignorant of it, other than defect of knowledge or of benevolence in the author.

Paley's point here is that he has in fact, applied abductive logic, and he believes his conclusion is quite reasonable. Looking at the amount of the world that is good, is it more likely to indicate a good designer or a bad one. The 'bad' bits might seem grim to us, but in fact, they may well need to exist – we just lack the understanding why. This point will be studied further in the 'Atheism' section of the Advanced Higher course, but it should be noted that theists have tried several ways to justify how suffering can exist alongside the God of Classical Theism. If they are successful, then perhaps Paley can keep his loving God.

Checking Understanding

1. Explain Hume's stance on the validity of the design argument. How does he suggest it leads to a flawed conception of God?
2. Paley proposed several assertions to defend his argument from Hume's criticisms. Can you summarize these assertions and evaluate their effectiveness in addressing Hume's points?

💡 Thinking Task

Imagine William Paley and David Hume met to take part in a debate today.

- Write an initial speech for each of them and then a second in which they are given the chance to rebut (defend) their initial argument.

Who do you think would win?

Scientific responses

Paley's argument is **abductive** in that it asks the reader to consider which is the more plausible option – a designer God, or chance. Of course, Paley wasn't aware of the Theory of Evolution, Paley published *Natural Theology* in 1802, and Darwin didn't publish *On the Origin of the Species* until 1859, but as we've discussed before, many have come to understand that Evolution answers how the world appears designed.

English astronomer, Fred Hoyle, in his 1981 book titled 'Evolution from Space' used an analogy to criticise the idea that Evolution was a plausible solution to the designer in the world. Hoyle put forth his own analogy, comparing 'a tornado sweeping through a junkyard and assembling a Boeing 747 from the materials' with the chance of obtaining even a single function protein by chance combination. If we were to accept Hoyle's presentation of evolution, then perhaps Paley's abductive point could still stand, however, in *The Blind Watchmaker*, Richard Dawkins called the Boeing 747 a 'memorable misunderstanding.' Dawkin's point is that one of the most persistent misconceptions about evolutionary theory is the notion that it suggests complex organs, such as eyes, arise solely "by chance."

Even under the most charitable interpretation, this perspective on adaptive evolution must be deemed deeply misguided. While genetic mutation is indeed integral to the process and is random in its effects, natural selection, by definition, involves the non-random survival and reproduction of individuals. Variation occurs randomly, but whether it is preserved depends on its impact on survival and reproduction within a particular environment. No serious evolutionary biologist in the past 150 years has proposed that the emergence of complex organs is merely the result of chance.

Past Paper Question 2023

'Gravity explains the motions of the planets, but it cannot explain who sets the planets in motion.'

To what extent do you agree with scientific responses to the teleological argument?

Note: For a question like this, the quote is simply there to prompt thought. You do not have to respond to it explicitly.

Past Paper Question 2022: Source Question

'There seems to be no more design in the variability of organic beings and in the action of natural selection, than in the way the wind blows.' Charles Darwin

(a) Describe what is meant by the argument from design. (5)

(b) Analyse this source. (5)

(c) Evaluate this source. (5)

Religious Responses

Creationism encompasses all beliefs attributing the origins of the universe and life to supernatural or miraculous means. In Christianity, creationism asserts that God created the world and everything within it from nothingness. Adherents of creationism hold that the Genesis account, found in the first volume of the Old Testament, offers the true narrative of the origins of the observable world. Genesis begins with the passage:

> *"In the beginning God created the heaven and the earth. And the earth was without form, and void; and darkness was upon the face of the deep. And the Spirit of God moved upon the face of the waters. And God said, Let there be light: and there was light."*

According to this account, the universe and its contents were created over a span of six days. On the initial day, God fashioned light and darkness. On the subsequent day, He formed the heavens, and on the third, He crafted the Earth's dry land and vegetation. God created the Sun and the Moon on the fourth day, followed by fish and birds on the fifth day, and land animals and humans on the sixth day.

Although the Genesis narrative serves as the foundation for Christian creationism, there exists a variety of interpretations within Christianity. For instance, a flat-earth creationist not only upholds the belief that God created the world ex nihilo but also asserts that the Earth is flat, stationary, and approximately 6,000 years old. Conversely, a progressive creationist acknowledges the findings of modern astronomy and geological dating methods, which suggest that the Earth is billions of years old, but rejects the conclusions of modern biology, maintaining that species can only evolve under the guidance of God.

Paley's teleological argument could be said to support both positions in that both creationists and Paley believe they have proof of a Creator. But we've noted before, Paley stipulated that he believed the existence of a creator, and a query about his attributes are separate questions. Paley did argue (in his 5th chapter) that he believed the many instances of good things in the world, should be held to outnumber the bad when considering God's nature. But did not go as far to innumerate the number of characteristics assigned to God as the Christian Bible. If one were to accept Paley has successfully proving a God, one could then read the Bible or other religious texts, in the belief that it would provide something more. But that would undoubtably be a step of faith rather than logic.

4 ARGUMENTS FROM INTELLIGENT DESIGN

Before we embark on arguments from intelligent design, we need to remember that they have been written with the knowledge of evolution. Unlike Aquinas who was writing hundreds of years before Darwin, or Paley who died 5 years before Darwin was born, the proponents of Intelligent Design know of the theory but believe that it is wrong or over-stated.

Michael Behe, a leading proponent of Intelligent Design, challenges the notion that evolution fully accounts for the complexity observed in the natural world. Behe's argument, known as "irreducible complexity," posits that certain biological structures are too complex to have evolved gradually through natural selection and mutation alone. Instead, he argues that these structures must have been designed by an intelligent agent.

This scepticism towards evolution as the sole explanation for biological complexity leads us to reconsider Darwin's theory in its most basic form. Evolution, as elucidated by Darwin, describes the biological process by which populations of organisms undergo genetic change over time. It involves mechanisms such as genetic variation, natural selection, and environmental influences that drive the diversification and adaptation of life forms on Earth.

Irreducible complexity, as proposed by Behe, suggests that certain biological structures are composed of multiple components, all of which are necessary for the structure to function. According to Behe, if any one of these components were to be removed or altered, the structure would cease to function, rendering it useless. Therefore, such structures could not have evolved gradually through a series of small, incremental changes, as proposed by evolutionary theory.

Behe often uses the bacterial flagellum as a prime example of irreducible complexity. The bacterial flagellum is a whip-like appendage used by bacteria for movement. Behe argues that the flagellum is composed of multiple parts, all of which are necessary for its function as a propulsion system. According to him, the flagellum could not have evolved gradually, as it would be non-functional without any one of its components.

Behe has attempted to illustrate his concept of irreducible complexity with an analogical argument:

A mousetrap consists of several essential components: a base, a spring, a hammer, a catch, and a holding bar. If any one of these components is missing or non-functional, the mousetrap cannot perform its function of catching mice. Behe argues that certain biological systems, such as the bacterial flagellum or blood clotting cascade, are similarly irreducibly complex. That is, they require the precise coordination of multiple components, and the removal of any one component would render the system non-functional.

The analogy may well seem like 'Paley in disguise' but it is worth noting some differences.

Evolutionists believe they have given Paley an answer for why natural organisms display 'apparent purpose' and view him as a product of his time – a reflection of scientific and philosophical discourse in the early 19th century. Behe is attempting to step in by arguing they have not been successful.

As a biochemist, Behe seeks to ground his arguments in scientific observations and principles. He argues that such systems could not have evolved gradually through natural selection because removing any one part would render the system non-functional. Behe is not saying that a mousetrap and nature are alike in function, rather that both are irreducibly complex and can only be explained by design.

Note that there is often a distinction made between the Intelligent Design movement and Theistic Evolutionists. While Theistic Evolutionists believe that God operates solely through natural processes, adhering to the notion that God's involvement is indirect, Intelligent Design proponents contend that God has directly intervened at specific junctures in natural history, deliberately bringing about particular features of the world.

For example, F.R. Tennant set out his anthropic principle in which he claimed that the entire universe was designed to produce human life one day. He based this claim on the idea that the conditions at the moment of the Big Bang must have been precisely set so that, 10 billion years later, our star would form and 5 billion years after that, our species would evolve. He is arguing for the universe to be able to come into being and then evolve, God is required. Behe would take issue with being grouped in with creationists, as he does agree that evolution exists. In his book *Darwin Devolves*,

Behe agrees that life has evolved over billions of years and that all living things share a common ancestry. He also acknowledges the role of mutation and natural selection in shaping organisms and improving their fitness in specific cases. However, he disagrees on how genetic changes - beyond minor tweaks - drive evolution. He maintains belief that a purposeful designer is needed in the development of complexity. He argues that a 'sculpting hand' is then needed for natural selection to be successful. For him, evolution is not the 'tool' because for him, he believes in God's continuing involvement not something that simply put a mechanism in place to work naturally.

Check your understanding

1. How does Michael Behe's concept of irreducible complexity challenge the traditional evolutionary understanding of gradual, incremental changes leading to the development of complex biological structures?

2. What are the key distinctions between the perspectives of Intelligent Design proponents like Behe and Theistic Evolutionists regarding the role of God or intelligent design in the natural world?

3. Can analogical arguments, such as Behe's comparison of biological systems to a mousetrap, effectively demonstrate the concept of irreducible complexity, or do they oversimplify the complexity of biological evolution?

Past Paper Question 2024

'Arguments from intelligent design fail to prove that God exists.' How far do you agree with this statement?

Philosophical responses

Behe's arguments have faced heightened scrutiny, partly due to a decision by the Dover, Pennsylvania school board mandating the inclusion of intelligent design in high school biology curriculum. Subsequently, eleven parents filed a lawsuit to block this policy, leading to the landmark trial Kitzmiller v. Dover in 2005. This trial marked the first direct challenge to a public school district policy in US federal courts. Michael Behe testified in this trial, resulting in intensified criticism of his arguments by opponents of teaching creationism and intelligent design in schools.

Among these opponents are physical anthropologist Eugenie Scott and Glenn Branch, the deputy director of the National Centre for Science Education. They raised a direct philosophical criticism, arguing that intelligent design proponents rely on arguments from ignorance. This critique aligns with previous criticism of teleological arguments, which often attribute gaps in knowledge to God without considering that such gaps may be filled through further understanding. The philosophical form of this critique is known as an argument from ignorance, where unverifiable explanations, often supernatural, are used to address unanswered questions.

Scott and Branch assert that intelligent design falls into this category by relying on gaps in knowledge to infer an intelligent cause. They argue that scientists typically view unanswered questions as opportunities for further exploration rather than as evidence for supernatural intervention. They also challenge Behe's insistence on increasingly detailed explanations for the historical evolution of molecular systems, suggesting that his approach creates a false dichotomy between evolution and design, with any perceived shortcomings in evolution being interpreted as victories for design. Additionally, Scott and Branch note that proposed contributions by intelligent design proponents have not led to significant scientific advancements.

American philosopher and cognitive scientist Daniel Dennett – who incidentally holds the accolade of being one of the 'horsemen' of New Atheism – also picked up on this criticism. He argued that Behe's concept of irreducible complexity presupposes a supernatural explanation and fails to adequately consider naturalistic evolutionary processes as potential explanations for complex biological systems. He suggested that young researchers are hesitant to tackle these gaps not because they fear a lack of evolutionary explanation, but because they anticipate discovering naturalistic explanations through further scientific exploration.[6]

---

[6] For more on Dennett's response check out his debate with Alvin Plantinga on this topic: https://isi.org/intercollegiate-review/a-marriage-made-in-heavenbr-a-review-of-emscience-and-religion-are-they-compatible-em-by-daniel-c-dennett-and-alvin-plantinga/

Scientific responses

Intelligent Design arguments, like Behe's, claim to be scientific but often face criticism as 'pseudoscience', suggesting they are more theological than scientific. Behe's own colleagues at Lehigh University went as far as publicly opposing his views, stating that Intelligent Design lacks scientific basis, experimental testing, and should not be considered scientific. Despite being described by his colleagues as 'generous and friendly', Behe himself acknowledges that without tenure, his survival in academia would have been unlikely.

The attention Behe's hypothesis garnered, particularly during the Kitzmiller v. Dover trial and debates on creationism in American schools, is largely attributed to external factors. During the trial, Behe encountered over 50 scientific publications refuting his examples of irreducible complexity, to which he responded dismissively, claiming they were insufficient or inadequately explained, and simply 'not enough.'

One such publication includes Michael LePage's article from New Scientist – he highlighted the diversity of flagella across species and the presence of components capable of independent functions. Contrary to Behe's claims, LePage suggests that the flagellum could have evolved gradually through mutation and selection rather than being designed. He discussed the possibility of the flagellum originating from pre-existing cellular systems, such as a protein export system or an ion-powered pump, adapting over time to serve propulsion functions. Furthermore, he emphasized that the inability to provide a complete evolutionary account right now does not prove the existence of design over evolution:

> *Think of a stone archway: hundreds of years after the event, how do you prove how it was built? It might not be possible to prove that the builders used wooden scaffolding to support the arch when it was built, but this does not mean they levitated the stone blocks into place. In such cases Orgel's Second Rule should be kept in mind: "Evolution is cleverer than you are."*[7]

---

[7] Michael Le Page, Evolution myths: The bacterial flagellum is irreducibly complex, New Scientist Magazine.
https://zephr.newscientist.com/article/dn13663-evolution-myths-the-bacterial-flagellum-is-irreducibly-complex/#:~:text=However%2C%20what%20has%20been%20discovered%20so%20far%20%E2%80%93,%E2%80%93%20show%20that%20they%20are%20not%20%20%E2%80%9Cirreducibly%20complex%E2%80%9D.

Some have tried to defend Behe's perspective by citing his Christian beliefs, but Behe insists that Intelligent Design is purely a scientific hypothesis, albeit with philosophical or religious implications. He acknowledges his belief in a designer, whom he identifies as God, though he maintains that science has not definitively answered the question of the designer's identity.

Critics of Intelligent Design are not necessarily godless atheists; many are devout Christians themselves. Their opposition stems from the overwhelming evidence supporting gradual development through natural, evolutionary processes. For believers, these processes are seen as manifestations of God's providence in ordering the world.

Religious responses

Just as some Christians are against the idea of Intelligent Design because it is unsupported by mainstream scientific thought, other Christians are against it because it contains too much science i.e. it accepts that Evolution is partly responsible.
Young earth creationists such as Ken Ham, adhere fervently to the belief that the Bible is not just a book of allegories or moral teachings but the literal word of God, infallible and without error. For them, the account of creation in Genesis is not a metaphorical narrative but a precise historical record. Thus, when the Bible states that God created the universe in six days, Ken

Ham and others like him assert that those were six literal, 24-hour days.

Ken Ham stands as one of the prominent figures in the realm of creationism, having founded "Answers in Genesis" and the Creation Museum in Kentucky. He champions the idea that any evidence, regardless of its source or perceived validity, must conform to the teachings of Scripture. In essence, if scientific findings – such as Behe's Intelligent Design theory - contradict the Bible, they are deemed invalid.

One of the cornerstones of Ken Ham's argument against evolution lies in the supposed gaps within the fossil record. He argues that these gaps invalidate the theory of evolution, as there is no conclusive evidence to bridge the apparent discontinuities in the evolutionary timeline. Additionally, Ken Ham criticizes the concept of natural selection, considering it a circular argument. While proponents of evolution argue that natural selection favours the survival of the fittest, Ham contends that survival itself becomes the criterion for fitness. Thus, in his view, natural selection fails to provide a satisfactory explanation for the diversity of life on Earth.

Another common refrain from Ken Ham and other creationists is the question: "If humans descended from monkeys, why are there still monkeys?" Ham posits that while evolution may account for microevolutionary changes within species, it falls short in explaining the emergence of entirely new species. He contends that the mechanisms proposed by evolutionary theory cannot adequately explain the complexity and diversity of life forms observed in the natural world as he says, 'Only elephants can come from elephants!'

Whilst he absolutely agrees with Behe that the complexity in the world necessitates a designer, he would not diverge from the Biblical narrative.

5 FINAL THOUGHTS AND REVISION NOTES

In the context of the early 18th Century, there was a rise in natural theology, attempting to infer God's existence and attributes from nature's order and complexity. By the mid-19th Century, however, religion and science had grown apart. Paley's argument was, in the words of Alistair McGrath, "the last stand of an intellectual movement in terminal decline". Paley's argument – although effectively communicated – represented an outmoded way of thinking. Even as Paley was writing his argument, most people had already accepted that natural theology cannot tell us one thing about Christianity proper. Paley's argument – to the dismay of many Christians now *and* then – traps Christianity in a pre-scientific worldview that can only end in disaster. It's important to note that the weaknesses of Paley's argument cannot be regarded – as some people do – as a refutation of Christianity. The weaknesses of Paley's arguments are simply a refutation of a wrong turn taken by the Church in the mid-19th Century. Paley is fascinating from a *historical* perspective – his argument tells us a lot about the 18th Century English worldview. All Dawkins has therefore achieved is to demonstrate the vulnerability of such historically-burdened approaches to the doctrine of creation. As McGrath argues that "Dawkins makes a superb case for abandoning Paley. Sadly, he seems to think this also entails abandoning God".

Darwin himself was generous in his account of Paley's argument. He noted his appreciation of Paley's "beautiful and reverent descriptions of the dissected machinery of life" – but perhaps that's all it is. Brian Clack argues that Paley's argument is not really a claim about the world itself but is, instead, an expression of *his view* of the world: "it is a statement about the *perceiver* rather than about the *perceived*". Clack argues that Paley's statements about the complexity and purpose of the universe are really just *projections* that provide metaphysical comfort i.e. a psychological explanation (Hume). What we have found in Paley's argument is *misapplied sentiment*. Paley's expression of delight about the world he lives in is perfectly natural, but he cannot legitimately move from that expression to a conclusion about the nature and being of God. Clack proposed that perhaps it should be viewed as a hymn of praise rather than a philosophical proof - as a hymn of praise it is very powerful; as an attempt at a proof, it fails.

It's also interesting to think about Emmanuel Kant's take on theology. He proposed that all *a posteriori* theistic 'proofs' must be rejected. No argument formulated within this world of sense experience can be used to convey us beyond this world to another. The key strength of the evolutionary explanation for the complexity and apparent purposefulness of the natural world (an explanation that fully accounts for the evidence without reference to God) is that the mechanism and its effects both lie within our field of experience while the design hypothesis invokes another realm. But don't forget that the evolutionary explanation cannot – for the same reason – disprove the God hypothesis. As Stephen Jay Gould said: "we neither affirm nor deny [God's existence]; we simply cannot comment on it as scientists." Having rejected the possibility of a theistic proof, Kant comes to the defence of believers and reminds them that religious conviction is – and should be – independent of any theoretical attempt to prove God's existence.

Revision notes

Some of the points below summarise the notes from this book, whereas others indicate thinkers/ideas that you may want to look at in class or as part of your own study. Remember, at Advanced Higher level, although there are mandatory bullet points there is a lot of freedom within those to examine any number of thinkers.

About the Argument ✓

- (P1) The world contains order, regularity, purpose, and beauty.
- (P2) By looking at an object containing these properties, we may infer that is was *designed*.
- (P3) The world is an object containing the properties in P1
- CONCLUSION: the world was designed; the designer we call 'God'
- 'Teleological' comes from teleos (Greek of purpose); it is concerned with how much of nature appears to work towards an end.
- The Argument is *a posteriori* (based on experience), **inductive** (probabilistic), **abductive** (deducing the best possible option out of those available), and in many instances **analogical** (dependent on a demonstration of resembles)

Aquinas: argument from design

- **Fifth Way** – from the governance of things – design *qua* regularity
- The Universe conforms to laws and recurrently does so.
- Such universality of temporal order suggests design.
- There must therefore be a designer (God).

Paley: argument from design ✓

- 1802 – Natural Theology
- We know that a watches complexity is explained by design.
- The universe too shows complexity – birds' wings, human eye, planetary motion.
- Like effects have like causes (analogy) so may infer origin of both is the same (designer).
- Universe infinitely more complex than watch so designer must be also. (God).

Argument: intelligent design ✓

- A group of scientists and mathematicians at the Discovery Institute have argued that Darwin was wrong about natural selection.
- The complexity of nature may be due to Intelligent Design.
- Michael Behe – organisms like the bacterial flagellum display 'irreducible complexity'. They have too many component parts to be explained through natural selection.

Hume's Criticisms ✓

- **The uniqueness of the Universe** – Universe is unique and therefore incomparable. Use of analogy inappropriate. Need to have other universes and to know of the origins of them. Additionally, whilst the **parts** of the universe we see may indicate order – cannot apply that to whole – or the parts we have not and cannot observe.
- **Diversity of causal explanation** – to claim that there can only be **one** explanation of design is the fallacy of the affirmation of the consequent. Universe could BE an animal or vegetable. Or Epicurean hypothesis – random revolutions of unguided matter...
- **Principle of proportionality** – let's use analogy... but properly. Ineffectual design indicates ineffectual design. Oh... damn.

Defence of Teleological Argument Against Hume

- Uniqueness does not preclude comparison. Without analogy we would be left with very little. The purpose of induction is to look at options and use the knowledge that we have.
- There may be diversity of causal explanation but that doesn't mean that God ISN'T the best option.
- This could come down to perspective – whilst design could appear 'red in tooth and claw' (Vardy) there could be a reason beyond our understanding. This *could* be the best system possible.

- Aquinas (certainly) and Paley to an extent could be understood as purporting their world view. Aquinas went on what he had to work with and therefore his induction is sound. His design is a modern thinker's evolution.

F.R. Tennant – Anthropic Principle ✓

- Humanity is at the forefront of creation, because the circumstances of the universe uniquely and surprisingly enable human life to emerge.
- P1) The emergence of human life in our universe depends on numerous factors: planetary conditions, fundamental laws of physics, etc.
- P2) Human life has emerged in our universe.
- P3) A life-friendly universe such as ours is highly improbable; almost any other set of circumstances we can think of would have been life-hostile.
- P4) A designer or intelligent Creator would make sense of our improbable universe.
- CONCLUSION: God exists

Criticism of Intelligent Design

- God of the Gaps – inductive leap – can't explain it – must be God!
- Watch vs vegetable. Bacteria vs mousetrap. **Organic cannot be compared to mechanic.**
- **Peter Atkins:** Multiverse theory – there may be and may have been many universes, most of which are chaotic and do not sustain life. Chance of an orderly universe: not remote.

- <u>Humans over-state their importance</u> –Mark Twain: The world was not created as an amazing habitat for man; man exists because of the world, not the other way around.
- **Brandon Carter:** We should not be surprised at how the universe is. If it were different, we would not be here.
- **Jacques Monod:** "Pure chance, absolutely free but blind, is at the very root of evolution."

Useful Quotes

Thomas Aquinas: 'We see that things which lack intelligence, such as natural bodies, act for an end, and this is evident from their acting always… in the same way, so as to obtain the best result.'

William Paley: 'This mechanism being observed… the inference, we think, is inevitable; that the watch must have a maker… who formed it for the purpose which we find it actually to answer; who comprehended its construction, and designed its use… every manifestation of design, which existed in the watch, exists in the works of nature.'

Hume as Cleanthes: 'Since therefore the effects resemble each other, we are led to infer, by all the rules of analogy, that the causes also resemble; and the author of nature is somewhat similar to the mind of man; though possessed of much larger faculties, proportioned to the grandeur of the work.'

Hume: 'the dissimilitude is so striking that the utmost you can pretend to is a guess.'

Hume: 'the eternal revolutions of unguided matter, and may not this account for all the appearing wisdom and contrivance, which is in the universe?'

Hume: 'We may never be allowed to ascribe to the cause any qualities but that are exactly sufficient to produce the effect.'

Keith Ward: "The argument in its seventeenth-century form … may have been superseded by Darwin. But the design argument still lives, as an argument that the precise structure of laws and constants that seem uniquely fitted to produce life by a process of evolution is highly improbable. The existence of a designer or creator God makes this much less improbable. That is the new Design Argument, and it is very effective."

Hugh Montifiore: "The distribution of gas in the universe from the big bang onwards had to be delicately balanced . . . without this fine balance, there would have been no galaxies, no stars, no planets, no life."

Dawkins: "life has the creative potential within itself and take the opportunity afforded it by genetic mutation to actualize its potential. God is not needed to explain this – it is self-explanatory."

Dawkins (simple summary of natural selection): "A theory of random mutations plus non-random cumulative selection."

McGrath (summary of Dawkins): "When the mechanism is understood, the very notion of 'purpose' had to be declared redundant."

Ingersoll (1884): "The doctrine of the origin of species has removed in every thinking mind the last vestige of orthodox Christianity."

Other reading

Particularly if you have chosen to study the teleological argument for your dissertation, the following sources may be of use.

Richard Swinburne. *The Existence of God*. (Oxford: Clarendon Press, 2004).

Michael Palmer. The Question of God. (New York: Routledge, 2002).

Jordan, Lockyer and Tate. *Philosophy of Religion for A Level*. (Cheltenham: Nelson Thornes, 2002).

Christopher Hamilton. *Understanding Philosophy for AS Level*. (Cheltenham: Nelson Thornes, 2003).

J.L, Mackie. *The Miracle of Theism*. (Oxford: Clarendon Press, 1982).

William Lane Craig and Quentin Smith. *Theism, Atheism, and Big Bang Cosmology* (Clarendon Press; 1993)

Peter Cole *Philosophy of Religion* (Hodder, 2002)

David Hume: Philosopher of Modern Science. (Oxford, Basil Blackwell, 1986)

Neil A. Manson. *God and Design: The Teleological Argument and Modern Science*. (Routledge, 2003)

Mel Thompson. *An Introduction to Philosophy and Ethics.* (Hodder Murray, 2007)

Nigel Warburton. *Philosophy, The Basics.* (Routledge, 2013)

Stanford Encyclopaedia of Philosophy
https://plato.stanford.edu/entries/teleological-arguments/

OTHER BOOKS IN THE ENLIGHTENED RMPS COLLECTION

National 5: Judaism

National 5: Existence of God

Higher: Islam

Advanced Higher: Atheism

Advanced Higher: Medical Ethics

All available on Amazon.

You can also find us on Instagram (@enlightenedrmps)

ABOUT THE AUTHOR

Laura Crichton is a teacher of Religious, Moral, and Philosophical Studies in Edinburgh. She gained her MA in Divinity at the University of Aberdeen, before completing her PGDE at the University of Edinburgh. She has taught Advanced Higher RMPS since 2009 and works for the Scottish Qualifications Authority - at both Higher and Advanced Higher. Before teaching, she served in the Royal Signals Corps and now is a CCF Army Officer. She enjoys teaching immensely - provided she has a cup of coffee in hand.

Printed in Great Britain
by Amazon